The Hitch Effect

Understanding The Value of An Equally Yoked Marriage

Esther Rising

Esther Rising Publisher

ERP

Publisher since 2012
P.O. Box 3672
Brentwood, TN 37024
615.935.2229

For more information, go to

Esther.Rising@gmail.com

EstherIsRising@instagram

https://www.facebook.com/esther.rising.1

www.estherrising.net

Interior Editor: India J Hunter

Cover Design: Esther Rising Publisher. Image by 123RP. Cover copyright ©2023 by Esther Rising Publisher

2nd Edition June 2023

Printed in the United States of America

ISBN 979-8-89121-724-9

ACKNOWLEDGEMENTS

This book is dedicated to my daughter India....phenomenal

woman....a Queen with a servant's heart.

A few words on why this book was written..

I love listening to and sharing relationship stories. Sometimes these stories are my own, sometimes they are stories I hear while in an airport, a restaurant, at an event, or someone I know. The point is, I listen and hear because it matters. Sometimes the relationship story is about a friendship, sometimes it is a business partnership, sometimes a dating experience with a significant other, and often, a marriage. And often, a failing or failed marriage. And often, marriage number two or three, or maybe five. And sometimes, a beautiful, thriving marriage of many years.

Of all the stories, my favorite is the marriage story. There are common threads in these stories. One of the most consistent threads are the questions *'How do I get this right?' 'Why didn't I get it right before?'* and *'How do I keep it right?'*

In response to these shared stories, I wanted to write about the Something that is hiding in plain sight. Not because it is complex, but because, if misunderstood, it is undervalued, or not valued at all. Hence, not modeled. That Something is being equally yoked in a marriage.

CONTENTS

ACKNOWLEDGEMENTS ... III

Chapter 1 ... 1

Chapter 2 ... 12

Chapter 3 ... 25

Chapter 4 ... 29

Chapter 5 ... 36

Chapter 6 ... 42

Chapter 7 ... 49

Chapter 8 ... 54

Chapter 9 ... 60

Chapter 10 ... 66

Chapter 11 ... 68

Chapter 12 ... 70

Chapter 13 ... 74

Chapter 14 ... 76

ENDNOTES ... 78

Chapter 1

What is it about being yoked equally in a marriage or not being yoked equally that keeps my attention? That keeps anyone's attention?

One major reason: The sincere desire to get married is coupled with a want to stay married – successfully and happily. Other questions that accompany the desire to marry are:

How do I know I'm ready for marriage?

How do I know who is the right person to marry?

How do I know how to be the type of spouse to help make the marriage fulfilling and complete?

What are the main reasons I want to marry?

What if I fail as a spouse?

What if my spouse fails as a spouse?

What if I marry the wrong person?

Do I really want to be with only one person for the rest of my life?

How do I have the benefits of marriage and keep them?

Can I remain single and still be as content as a successfully married person?

How do so many marriages fail?

How do successfully married people stay married?

What married couples should be chosen as role models?

How do know I am financially ready to get married?

What is the purpose or highest calling for my life? Will my spouse support it?

These are more than a few frequently asked questions when marriage is a consideration and goal. But note that most of the questions above start with 'How?' or 'What?' meaning there is a need for instructions and better understanding about getting and being married. And not just doing it, but doing it successfully. More simply, being married in a manner that sustains contentment in one's life, and in the life of their spouse for the duration of life together.

One of the ways answers are sought for the questions above is from models presented – positive and negative.

They are accepted as blueprints to follow.

The spiritual blueprint to have and keep an equally yoked marriage is different in many ways from that of the blueprint presented in much of our media culture. Often, in media, the path to have the best of marriage is void of most of the steps needed. In numerous cases, the path displayed will result in the opposite – an unequally yoked union. It is not uncommon to see the spiritual path needed to have an equally yoked marriage being presented as negative in media, or people who practice this path being ridiculed or diminished publicly. In contrast, some of the unhealthiest and unequally yoked marriages are sensationalized and placed on a public pedestal as an example to follow, or just for entertainment.

Compounded with the confusion in the personal lives of people about what is an equally yoked marriage, negative media messages can further endorse misunderstanding. And, naturally, people of all ages are influenced. As a result, they have painfully experienced the lows of a significant relationship and/or marriage that was not equally yoked. Sometimes these decisions become cyclic. Hence, marriage can become unattractive, a thing not to do.

When actually, an unequally yoked marriage is the thing not to do. This message becomes increasingly clear when growing numbers of people experience an equally yoke marriage and the unlimited positive fruits of it.

These equally yoked marriages are not only what God wants, but are exemplary to all.

They are profound.

This is The Hitch Effect.

Being equally yoked means not only being with the spouse with whom one can be content and want to stay married to for life, but being equally yoked comes with instructions that sustain a couple's union in an optimal way. Yes, a true guide exists for what this kind of marriage looks like every day, how to enter it, the benefits, what challenges to expect, how to successfully go through life trials together, the roles of the husband and wife, having peace and friendship in the marriage, what is really meant by 'until death do us part', and much more.

Being unequally yoked means the opposite for a couple. And there are descriptions on what this kind of marriage looks like every day, and how to avoid it.

Before discussing being equally yoked in deep dive style, Reader, simply put – being equally yoked means:

As a single person, you became a Christ believer (Christian). As a believer, you matured, and then decided to allow Jesus to be Lord of your heart – to agree and live the choices that go with that decision. Your spouse did the same.

You trust, ask for and accept God's response about the best spouse for you. Your spouse did the same.

You and your spouse agree with God for your marriage and commit to follow His instructions to keep it equally yoked for the rest of your lives together.

You and your spouse best complement each other's life purpose and are fully committed to helping each other carry it out.

Your strengths AND weaknesses strengthen the union.

Reader, there is an elephant in the room. Did you expect this definition of being equally yoked to be so simple? If it is so simple, then why are so many people divorced? Unhappily married? Why have a number of single people given up on being married? Why are there so many negative messages about marriage? Why are there not more positive examples of marriages visible in the media?

Before you disconnect, before you think being equally yoked is just an ideal and not obtainable, just stay plugged in long enough to understand. Because there are reasons that many people do not know how to have an equally yoked marriage. Therefore, it may appear as if the instructions needed are hiding in plain sight.

The purpose of this book is to help make the instructions be more in plain sight.

Suppose you desire to marry and want to be equally yoked. A logical question is: 'How does this happen?' So, there is an openness, a commitment to learn.

And as a next step, you agree to be yoked with Jesus first. And when you decide to yoke with Jesus, you begin to know Him in an every day way, not just a fleeting way. He rubs off on you. He not only shows you how much He loves you, but most importantly, through His example of depending on and interacting with His Father God, He lets you see how much God wants this same intimate relationship with you. Following Jesus' example, you start spending time with God, because you have been invited, and it is so much more comfortable to do so. You start acting like God, your Creator, and friend, more and more, mainly because of how He knows how to relate to and love you, custom style. This is one main reason Jesus said in the scripture that yoking with Him was easy. He was humble of heart like His dad Jehovah(more personal name), God. So, when you are learning about His humility and you draw closer to Jehovah because of it, you increasingly experience God in intimate, life giving, and loving ways.

Experiences like……

He spends more time listening to you than talking.
Jeremiah 29: 12-13; John 16:24

He views you differently, in a sacred way, because He
sees inwardly and loves you, like no other.
Jeremiah 17:10

He is open to you asking for help, advice.
Isaiah 41:10

He gives compliments.
Matthew 10:29-31; 1 Peter 2:9

He confronts prejudices.
Galatians 3:28; Matthew 7: 1-5; Acts 10:34

He asks questions.
Job 38-39

He answers your questions.
James 1: 5-6; Jeremiah 33:3; Psalm 91:15

He accepts your setbacks and challenges, as well as
your complaints about them, and offers solutions.
Psalm 73: 3, 13, 16,17, 24, 26

He shows you how to remain teachable.
Proverbs 22:4; Ephesians 4:2-3; 2 Chronicles 7:14

He embraces simplicity; is clear and consistent.
Malachi 3:6; Hebrews 13:8

He comforts you.
2 Corinthians 1:3-4

He loves spending time with you.
James 4:8; Jeremiah 29:13

He is sensitive to your needs.
Matthew 6:31-33; Philippians 4:6

He defends you.
Psalm 62:5-7; Isaiah 41:10

He protects you.
Psalm 91

He is truthful with you.
Psalm 145:18; John 18: 37-38; John 14:26

He sees you as a sibling of His son Jesus, and a friend.
Matthew 12:46-50; John 15: 1, 5, 12-14, 16

He does not shame or reject you.
Romans 10:11-12

He respects you.
Psalm 138:6; Romans 2:11

He holds you in the highest esteem.
Psalm 8: 3-6; Genesis 1:27

He is readily available.
1 Corinthians 10:13; Psalm 121: 1-8

He teaches you how to love.
1 Corinthians 13:4-8a

And these qualities build trust, encourage, and give life. Makes you want to be like Him. He helps you trust Him and see Him as not only your Creator, but a Father who will not fail you.

Picture it. A yoke, as we know it, is a wooden bar which connects two oxen(or two animals) by the neck so they can pull a load attached to a cross bar on the yoke. The more the animals agree to work together, the easier it is to pull the load successfully and move farther.

The analogy of being equally yoked (or not) is used to explain how a husband and wife in marriage team up to navigate life loads. So compare the wooden yoke on the neck of animals to a symbolic yoke of agreement the couple makes to love each other and go through life together until death do them part.

Straightforward, huh?

Then why did Jesus say "For *My* yoke is easy, and *My* burden (or load) is light (Matthew 11:30)?" Why does He speak of **His** yoke and burden as if it is a better option?

Picture it. He says it's His yoke – not your yoke.

The yoke He speaks of is attached to Him. So, to whom is Jesus attached? Yes, His Father, God. His Father is the Lord of His heart. He follows the lead of His Father in all circumstances. When we agree to let Jesus be the Lord of our heart, we agree to trust the example He sets to follow His Abba (meaning father in the most intimate way) Father, God. We trust them to lead, teach, love, instruct, cover, heal, and protect us through every life circumstance. So the yoke Jesus carries for us *IS* easy compared to the earthly, man-made, or more specifically, limited yoke.

Likewise, His burden is light. Because the way He leads us through life gives us life, peace, and understanding of our trials and good times. It gives us continual clarification of our God given purpose and the ability to fulfill it. This is the abundant life God promised we experience as we put Him first and remain in intimate relationship with Him.

Envision Jesus literally taking the yoke and burdens on Himself as He asks us to trust and follow Him through our life and grow closer to Him and God.

Isaiah 10:27 clarifies "In that day, his (man-made) yoke shall be taken away from off your shoulder and his yoke from off your neck; and the yoke shall be destroyed because of the anointing oil."

Reader, the anointing oil was used to acknowledge (in a visible, human way) the supernatural intervention and evidence of God in our lives, or the anointing of God.

So, the equally yoked marriage part. Picture it.

First, a single man, the husband to be has been living in agreement that Jesus is Lord of his heart. His life and behavior consistently reflect this decision in his single season.

First, as a single woman, the wife to be has been living in agreement that Jesus is Lord of her heart. Her life and behavior consistently reflect this decision in her single season.

When they marry, they are joined in holy matrimony, both committed to continue following the example of Jesus in their lives together until death. The agreement is sustained by the anointing of God. Fulfilling God's scriptural promise in Matthew 19:6: "Therefore, what God has joined together, let no man put asunder."

How again? "My yoke is easy; My burden is light."

Before the discussion about being equally yoked (or not) goes into more detail, I am going to share what I knew as a very young women about who to marry and being married.

I am also going to share some stories others have shared with me about their unequally yoke marriages. Just some every day stuff we tend to hear about.

Chapter 2

Some of my early story...

I remember from my very early dating days I had strong ideas about what I did not want in a relationship with a boyfriend.

And things I wanted at an early age...

I was keenly aware when a young man wanted me. I was quietly cool and confident. And emotionally comfortable with one man at a time. I hated and still hate infidelity.

My daddy was very masculine. A manly man. So, I loved this quality in young men my age.

I wanted the young man to lead. I was taught not to chase them.

I was taught not to sleep with a young man before marriage. I believed this practice was right for other reasons besides religion. What was most motivating for me not to cross the line – I didn't want to get pregnant and break my parents' heart. I wanted to go to college and having a pregnancy would interfere with this plan.

So, I put thought into how I could work around the sex, and still be sexual with a boyfriend. There was no GPS for this process, no discussion with parents about it, maybe a little talk with girlfriends. But mainly trial and error.

More things I knew I wanted...

Daddy was good looking, so my boyfriend had to be good looking.

Daddy had a sense of humor, so my boyfriend had to have that quality, too.

Daddy was athletic, so the athletic type was attractive to me, though not a must.

And he had to be a good enough guy on the inside to win my daddy's approval. And that was not easy.......
because………..

I was the apple of my daddy's eye.

And I knew my daddy would…...

Protect me.

Support me.

Brag about me.

Sacrifice for me.

Work hard to provide for me.

Give his life for mine.

So, this gave me a no-nonsense approach without thinking about it much. I knew I couldn't bring just anybody home.

And though this road map had several positive attributes, it was a very rough and vague GPS for helping me decide who was the best friend, boyfriend, fiancé, husband. It was not enough. It did not clearly define what an equally yoked or unequally yoked relationship looked like.

I learned the difference in very hard and painful ways. I learned what an unequally yoked relationship was first. My experience is not unique. What do I mean?

Well, it helps to share some stories of couples who didn't have it figured it out, like me. Stories of being unequally yoked, but not understanding why, or what to do about it. Before we continue with a deeper look at what are equally yoked marriages, let's consider some stories I will share of unequally yoked marriage and relationships and the outcomes...

<u>Couple 1</u>

I met an awesome man, about 50 years old, who had been highly successful in his career. He had achieved the heights of notoriety as a professional athlete. He had recently left a job with a six-figure salary to pursue his ministry full time. One of his passions was to teach athletes, younger and older, how to live practically as godly men in a career atmosphere full of the opposite messages. He was financially capable of achieving this transition comfortably. But shortly after this transition began, he and his wife separated. He expressed sadness about how angry and disappointed his wife was with his decision to pursue ministry full time. Their separation and her disapproval were obviously a source of great pain and discomfort for him amidst his apparent joy and contentment to finally live in his God calling fully. And he was relieved to not hide anymore, and to have total peace. He and his wife had been married close to ten years. He said they had been separated for several months, and the separation began about three months after he started full time ministry and began growing more intimate in his relationship with God.

He expressed how this intimacy and alone time with God showed him his pride and selfishness, and he wanted to be free of it.

He said prior to the transition, he and one of his sons were estranged due to his waywardness and selfish agenda over several years. Following his surrender to and agreement with God to fully follow His plans versus his own, he and his son reconciled and are now closer than ever. His son became one of his biggest fans in encouraging him to continue in this transformation.

So now he is walking in total peace, yielding to his highest calling, his life purpose. And though amid a separation from his wife, he could plainly see the marriage would be reconciled by them becoming equally yoked. However, if the marriage remains unequally yoked, it would end.

His resolve to stay the course in the marriage was born out of much pain. This was his second marriage. He admitted the responsibility for the end of the first marriage was his fault – pride, selfishness, infidelity, partying, strife, and depression – all at the height of his career. And he was also unequally yoked in the first marriage.

And during the second marriage, even with a greater commitment to not make the same mistakes he made in the first marriage, and a greater commitment to ministry, he confessed he was still living without full commitment to being a godly man, husband, father, and leader.

One way he knew he was doing this was because he drank. Though not an alcoholic, he was drinking to deny the fact that he had not fully accepted the highest calling on his life. He was still lord of his own life versus being yoked to Jesus fully, allowing Jesus to be the Lord of his heart. So, when that reality would hit him, he drank to deal with the anger he felt, the torn feelings, anxiety, frustration, fear, disappointment. And his wife noticed.

And God noticed.

He said as his desire to spend more intimate time with God became increasingly important to him, it became easier to stop drinking. Then the six-figure salary job started to become a distraction to his desire to do ministry full time. And over a three-month period, he sat in the parking lot a long time each day he went to work. He became increasingly sensitive to the immorality and injustices in his workplace because he was changing and hungering to fulfill the most important purpose for his life. So, he resigned. Three months later, he and his wife separated. Several months afterwards, they remained separated.

Does this sound familiar? What is happening here? Well, to understand more, let's look at what was happening before the separation.

Husband and Wife are....

Believers

Financially stable

Committed to being parents (both had children before they married)

Career driven

Same social circle

Same social interests

Communicating as spouses

After separation

| *Husband* | *Wife* |

Husband	Wife
Believer	Believer
Financially stable	Financially stable
Committed to being parents	Committed to being parents
Ministry driven	Career driven

Priority is seeking intimate time with God	Not clear
Varied social circle	Same social circle
Some changes in social interests	Same social interests
Little or no communication with spouse	Little or no communication with spouse

Prior to this transition, the couple was yoked based on similar goals they had for their lives – primary focus on career, social circles, and parenting. This is not negative goal setting for a marriage. But neither understood the critical step for both to prioritize together the constant intimacy needed with God, and to collaborate as they fulfill the highest calling for their life. It was not a focus before this crisis. And it is apparent the wife is not in agreement with the new direction her husband has taken. Maybe she doesn't trust it? Maybe she is confused? Maybe she doesn't want to be the wife of a minister? Maybe the relationship was yoked based on who both thought they were...

We will come back to this story...

For now, let's look at another unequally yoked marriage...

<u>Couple 2</u>

Based on her testimony, the wife said her spiritual parents did not want her to marry her first husband. She was determined to marry him, and she did. He became abusive in the marriage, after the birth of their child. She remembers hiding in the closet, asking God to get her out of the marriage. She promised to listen to Him going forward. And she did.

When the wife went back home to her parents after her first marriage ended, she completely dedicated herself to God. Giving Jesus Lordship of her heart. She and her child healed quickly, and she remained celibate during this time – gladly. She only wanted who God wanted for her in a spouse.

After three years, she meets the man who will be her second husband. About her second husband? He was a believer, had been married two times and both marriages were unequally yoked. He also had children from both marriages. So, let's pause for a short table shot of them....

Him	*Her*
Believer	Believer
Married twice previously	Married once previously
4 children	1 child
Not equally yoke in either marriage	Not equally yoked in prior marriage

When she met her future husband, he exceeded all expectations she had for a spouse. He told her on their first date she would be his wife. Following, she asked him to meet her spiritual parents because she didn't want to invest in a relationship they would not bless. She realized as much as she was into this man, her spiritual parents could say no to this man, too. And this time, she was willing to accept their response.

But her spiritual parents gave their blessing. And they married. A powerfully, equally yoked couple. Walking in and fulfilling their divine calling every day. Content. So, what was the difference here?

We will come back to this story, too...

Next story...

<u>Couple 3</u>

He had been married before. He was a believer when he married his high school sweetheart. But the marriage did not last.

So, he decided that he would seek God continually about who should be his wife. And he waited for the answer.

His next wife?

She had not been married when they met. She was previously engaged to her child's father, but the relationship did not last long after the birth of their child. She was a believer but matured spiritually in a great way through her breakup with her child's father.

After they met and married, he expressed that he saw her before he met her, and he knew he would marry her before he met her. Both said they prayed fervently and consistently for their future spouse after their breakups. She said she prayed every day with a prayer partner and close female friend. They both said in response to their prayers, God gave them clarity about the characteristics of their future spouse, what they needed, and they knew that their spouse had to align with their highest calling for God. Both knew soon after they met that they would marry. They are equally yoked and flourishing as a couple and family.

Let's return to this story later...

How familiar are these stories to you? Are they relatable? Are they realistic to you? Why or why not?

A takeaway before we go on...

Being equally yoked excels you both in your divine purpose from God, even through your trials together. Your strengths and weaknesses push one another to continual higher levels with God which is the most fulfilling life.

Being unequally yoked distracts and takes both away from your divine purpose for God, even in the better times together. Your strengths and weaknesses keep one another from higher levels with God, which is not a fulfilling life.

Let's talk about another relationship story.

<u>Couple 4</u>

The first marriage...

A bond formed in youth, innocence, and considerable naiveté. And though the couple is young, their sincerity pushes them toward desiring truth in the relationship, so there could be an equal yoking, but they may not be aware of it or how to maintain it.

And because they don't understand the value of an equally yoked marriage, as the years go on, they start to covet the attributes of an unequally yoked marriage. They start thinking the grass is greener on the other side, in a relationship that appears to be better than their own.

They begin to grow apart. They divorce to the surprise of many around them.

Second marriage...

Because of what they went through in the first marriage, often they highly value relationship, marriage, and family. But they are severely broken due to the failure of their first marriage. They are often heartbroken and sometimes realize that the first marriage was more worthy of the fight they could have done to keep it. So, they quickly began to focus on replacing the first marriage with the second marriage but are still trying to understand what was missing in the first marriage. They are still not understanding what an equally yoked marriage is, or what they had.

This situation is wide open for a rebound second marriage. An unequally yoked marriage. More wounds on unhealed wounds. In many cases, these second marriages fail, or remain but are unfulfilling. Sometimes the spouse who desired the marriage more is committed to stay in it, if only to keep from having another failed marriage.

Hence, the two either end the marriage quickly, or live in a very unhappy marriage, more as roommates versus husband and wife.

Have any of these stories hit a spot with you yet? Hmmmmmmmmm……….

Note to Reader: Going from unequally yoked to equally yoked – not a desired route, but possible. And common.

Another story...

<u>Couple 5</u>

A couple meets, starts dating, have great chemistry, effective communication, gets serious, and then a pregnancy.

They are committed to each other, so a breakup is not an option. They may or may not want to marry. The challenges of having a baby and family so soon in the relationship are hard. And the day-to-day responsibilities give them even less time to dedicate to the strengthening of the foundation of their relationship. So, they struggle, but are in it to win it. Not knowing or having little knowledge of what it is to be equally yoked. And although they want their relationship to last, they know something is missing.

This makes them hungry for more. But more of what? Sometimes it takes years. Sometimes more children are born. More disappointment. More challenges. Then they finally break to the point they seek God Jehovah desperately and consistently until they know the 'What' that is missing. In this hunger, they began to learn what an equally yoked union is, likely in bits and pieces, but their desire to learn more keeps them in God's face as he shows them. And though their initial foundation must be torn up for it be rebuilt, they do the very difficult work this requires, and they become equally yoked. So, their latter years together become greater than their former years.

If this sounds romantic, that is not the intent of this writer. It's victorious, but not the preferred route, and extremely hard to achieve.

But possible.

<u>Couple 6</u>

What about the couple whose relationship goal in a marriage is like their parents?

Often, they stay together for many years. If they are equally yoked, this is great. But let's say they are not equally yoked, and the marriage is a façade. An arrangement, though well intentioned in the beginning. They stay to raise the kids, to have good retirement income, to pay off a mortgage, for good community status. But there is no or little intimacy in the marriage. And sooner or later, the masks come off, and the foundation crumbles.

And the denial of being unequally yoked can go on for many years, just because the couple has accepted it. Until at least one spouse gets real, tells the truth about the marriage, and begins to seek God for the desired marriage – the qualities of an equally yoked marriage. Sometimes this means the current marriage will end. Sometimes this leads to the current marriage starting again as an equally yoked one.

What is it to be equally yoked, and how do we get there?

Chapter 3

What is an equally yoked marriage? What does it look like? Why is it so important?

Well, let's look at each part of the term, and what it means......

Equally means:

Symmetrically

Coordinately

Proportionately

Impartially

Fairly

Equitably

Yoked means:

> Attached
>
> Combined
>
> Coupled
>
> Connected
>
> Wed
>
> United
>
> Tied
>
> Secured
>
> Hitched
>
> Fastened

A refresher – a yoke is a wooden crosspiece that is fastened to the necks of two animals (load carrying species, like oxen, horses, etc.). It is attached to the plow or cart so the animals can pull it together. The yoke connects the animals for alliance, to move a load more successfully.

According to bible scripture reference Matthew 11:28-30, Jesus said...

"Come to me, all you who labor and are heavily burdened, and I will give you rest. Take My yoke upon you and learn from Me. For I am meek and lowly in heart (humble), and you will find rest for souls. For My yoke is easy, and My burden (some load pulled, carried, moved) is light."

What exactly was Jesus talking about in the scripture above?

An example of a burden can be worry, sadness, trauma, life responsibility, trial, etc.…

And maybe at this point, some questions are, what does a person, marriage, or Jesus have to do with:

Animals?

Yokes?

Burdens?

It is an invitation from Him to us as individuals to know Him, learn about Him intimately, yoke with Him. To submit ourselves to His authority. His leadership. To allow ourselves to be under His rule, His care, His Lordship, to surrender to and join with Him. He is inviting each of us to put our shoulders into a new yoke, one in which He is the yoke mate, one in which He is at the center. The yoke He carries.

Those words, to many, sound like giving up control to somebody or something about which they know nothing. Being completely vulnerable to someone or something they don't know enough about to trust. And all that feeling is understandable. Before you run away, consider the description of Jesus as Lord and His example to trust the lead of His Father God in the first chapter. Breathe and picture it again. . .

If we need help beyond our single selves to live life and be our best consistently, we need help beyond ourselves to marry and stay married in a healthy way. We need help beyond human limits to walk with another person through what life brings. We need help to grow with one another, remain true, and be our best person.

We need help when we are not our best person. When we are honest, we acknowledge we cannot successfully pull all the burdens of life by ourselves.........

Chapter 4

Going back to that introduction about being yoked with Jesus. About yoking with Jesus as a prior step to being equally yoked with your spouse – Remember the results? Those intimate experiences with God that give life. Those qualities that create trust, safety, longevity, respect. Qualities that nurture, sustain relationship, and reassure that it is safe to act the same way.

But you realize you cannot possibly keep this up all day, every day. Not with all life brings. Exactly. And He knows that, too. So, Jesus's invitation to yoke with us is not just about what is described above. It's also about letting Him pull those life burdens with you. It is about allowing Jesus to empower us by His example of leaning on and trusting His Father Jehovah. It is about trusting His rule in our heart and our life. That thing called Lordship.....

What is Lordship? This word brings up many images, some of which are negative, depending on your life, family, or even ethnic history. It is a severely misunderstood word – for understandable reasons. So don't run or shut down….

Well, for starters, let's look at the way the word 'lord' has been used historically.

According to Oxford Dictionary of English[1], the word lord is traced back to the old English word hlaford, which originated from hlaweard, meaning 'loaf ward' or 'bread keeper.' An additional source – Etymonline[2] - defines hlaford as 'master of a household', 'ruler', 'feudal lord', 'superior.'

In old English, lord is someone or something having power, authority, or influence over others. A ruler by hereditary right or preeminence to whom service, and obedience are due: one of whom a fee or estate is held in feudal tenure. An owner of land, property, and/or houses. A titled nobleman or peer.

More synonyms are……

Master of household

Ruler

Feudal lord

Superior

Husband

One who guards and distributes the loaves
Keeper
Guardian

Owner of land (landlord) or people

Nobleman under the rank of a duke and to a bishop from 1540s

Are you sweating yet? Because most of the above is quite different from the descriptions of Jesus or God referenced in earlier chapters. So, there is valid reason for the confusion about 'lordship.'

Should we use another term about this Lordship of the heart with Jesus and Jehovah God? We can. But is it necessary to understand it's different from the earthly definition of lord and lordship.

Let's talk some more about it.

Here are some different names for God, as referenced in scripture:

Adonai

Yhwh (Yahweh)

Adonai Elohim – The Lord God

Abba Avinu (Aramaic) – Our Father(most intimate)

Jehovah – God's personal name

Lord

All these words are equivalent to Jehovah God, the One who is the Creator and the father of Jesus. So, yielding to Jesus as Lord really means we agree with Him about who He yields to – His Father, His Creator, who is our Father, Our Creator. Right? Because Jesus sees us as His sibling, children of His Father – Right?

So, agreeing Jesus is Lord of our heart is also allowing the Lord God to be sovereign.

Uh, oh. Sovereign sounds like one of those control, power, maybe oppressive words…. again. But do you really know what it means?

Let's look closely. It means:

Leader

King

Majesty

Ruler

Queen

Great

Super

Supreme

Highest

Chief

Principal

Over

Absolute

Royal

Power

Very good

Effective

Above

Saying yes to yoke with Jesus is saying to yes to His Father Jehovah being first in your life. It means trusting

Jehovah God, above yourself and everything else. God is spirit Jesus came to earth as His son as a perfect man to surrender himself in full obedience to His Father God and complete the work of salvation from sin we need to live eternally. He did this through his crucifixion, taking victory over all the enemies or evils in sin, through his resurrection. So, in the earth, because Jesus completed this greatest act of love for us, He is Lord (versus lord) in earth and heaven, according to His Father God. After we agree to accept Jesus as our Savior, we are invited to give Him Lordship of our heart, yoking to Him, and to imitate his example of obedience to His Father God, who is also our Father God or Jehovah. God already knew we could not do this life in our own strength.

It means we trust God's appointment of his Son to set the example on how to live in a way to not only keep from destroying ourselves, but to know how to live in the best way, and eternally.

Notice this is an individual decision.

And simply put, sometimes there is confusion because Lord and lord, as explained in this chapter, are two different things.

What makes Jesus as <u>Lord</u> of our heart different from the traditional meaning of <u>lord</u>?

Jesus is **Lord** on this Earth (because he emptied Himself of all heavenly position, became flesh like us, died to conquer our sin, and was resurrected by his Father Jehovah to return to His heavenly position). The whole time on earth, Jesus continued to say He followed only His Father's wishes, He did only as His Father does, and

His actions confirmed His obedience. His Father, who created Him, is Spirit, Lord and Creator of heaven and earth, and cannot be housed in a body. Jesus was the first creation, before any man or woman was made. He and His Father Jehovah, work together.

To agree that Jesus is Lord in heaven and earth, in your heart, and life, is to honor Him for who He is, trust him, and surrender to His rulership. It means to follow His example. After all, He follows the best of the best. He has no sin but sacrificed His life so we can overcome our sin. He is divinely yielded, agreeably restrained, and obedient to Jehovah, His Father and Lord. According to John 5:19, "Very truly, I tell you, the Son can do nothing by himself. He can do only what he sees his Father doing, because whatever the Father does, the Son does also." Forever giving life.

In comparison, to agree that a <u>lord</u> in the earth is also <u>lord</u> of our heart is tempting, not only because of life familiarities, but because there can be associated positive qualities depending on our experience. But this lord is limited, circumstantial, temporary, flawed. This lord does not solely rely on the Creator God for the best instructions in all life circumstances. Therefore, this lord can and will fail (intentional or not intentional), particularly at the times we are most in need of help, causing despair, which takes life.

And when this heartbreak occurs, who is there to restore life? The Lord Jesus and His Father God.

So, much of what the above is about is the decision an individual makes, or a single person.

Are you still thinking what does this have to do with marriage, or are we going to talk about couples again? Understood. We're getting there...

Chapter 5

If the Father Jehovah, also known as Lord of Lords, Adonai, Abba Avinu.......is so awesome, why do so many choose not to trust Him, and do not agree that Jesus is Lord in the earth, heaven, in the heart? Why do so many not yoke to Jesus, his humanity and divinity, to teach and help us to live victoriously over sin? Why do so many not trust the One who knows us better than we know ourselves, the One who created us, who loves us more than anyone else?

Because many have a misperception and mistrust of Jehovah and Jesus often based on wrong teaching, limited understanding, life disappointments and traumas. Both are viewed through these filters, and it is damaging. It results in us putting our trust in what we think will give us the best life, which keeps us chasing and wanting an illusion. Rather than give life, this chase steals life.

For many, before adulthood, often before marriage, there is some heartbreak, some hardship, some negative spiritual experience, which lowers our confidence in Jehovah God, and the common reaction is to question any act of His, including sending his son Jesus to this earth. The truth about Jehovah and Jesus can all seem like a fairy tale, a lie, after some of these experiences.

Many things can and often do cause great confusion, and a lowered confidence in Jehovah and his plan of salvation for our lives. **Do any of these apply to you?**

Distrust of one or both parents

Unforgiveness of someone close who had our trust and violated us

Rebellion and acceptance of what we think is better or easier to trust (trust in idols)

Foundational teaching about Jehovah is incorrect. Mainly based on fear, judgement, lack of clarity, ignorance, and manipulation

Loss of loved one and unresolved grief

Experiencing or witnessing violence

Common types of traumas, such as ....

• Abuse – neglect, sexual, mental, emotional, societal (racism, sexism, classism), poverty

• Death – premature, illness or accident related

• Abandonment – by a parent, spouse, significant loved one

Let's zoom in on the influences listed above for more clarity.

Distrust of one or both parents due to:

• Immaturity of parent(s)

• Not being well (mental health problems, chronic illness, substance abuse)

• Being hostile with each other and using children as pawns

• Lack of good character

• Making other things more important than children (work, relationships, hobbies, money)

• Being too harsh or critical consistently

• Generational trauma and its effect on family

• Being absent, physically, emotionally, or both

Unforgiveness of someone close or their unforgiveness of us.......

• Parent

• Spouse

• Friend

• Pastor

• Sibling

• Foster Parent

• Authoritative figure

Rebellion and to accept what one thinks is better or easier than trusting Jehovah

• Valuing money, status, material things, relationships above relationship with God

• Rejecting the divine purpose of one's life

Foundational teaching about Jehovah is incorrect

• God is a taskmaster

• God is a slave master

• God is unforgiving

• God was not present, especially in troubled times

• God stood and watched me be violated and did nothing to stop it

• God is not real

• God is white or a color other my color

• God is not a protector

• God is in heaven, far from earth, and very distant, unreachable

• God does not want to hear my problems

• God is just like a bad parent(s)

• God can let you down

• Not sure God is real based on what I experienced

• God is limited

• God loves conditionally, just like humans

• God is for others, but not for me

• I do not deserve God's love and attention because I am imperfect

Loss of loved one and related unresolved grief

• Being in a natural disaster and/or losing loved ones, way of life, in a natural disaster

• Losing a loved one who was chronically ill

• Losing a loved one due to an accident

• Losing a loved one who was very young

• Being orphaned or widowed

• Losing a parent

• Losing a spouse

• Losing a close friend

Experiencing or witnessing violence

• Seeing someone murdered

• Experiencing domestic violence

• Being oppressed and a target of and violence due to race, ethnicity, sex, religious belief, economic class, sexual practices

• Being a part of a civil war

• Experiencing sexual violation

Experiencing Trauma

• Abuse – neglect, sexual, mental, emotional, societal (racism, sexism, classism), poverty

• Death – premature, illness or accident related

• Abandonment – by a parent, spouse, significant loved one

• Generational trauma

If any of the above resonated with you, do you see how much of our trust of God, and decision to agree with Him is impacted so much? And a lot of times at young ages? As a result, for any you checked, did you decide to yoke with Jesus fully, partially, or not at all before marriage based on the influences (and others) listed above?

If so, you are not alone.

Chapter 6

Getting back to the question - What does this have to do with marriage?

What goes on with us as a single person can continue in a marriage. What we yoke with before marriage can continue in a marriage.

This is the Hitch Effect.

If we are not equally yoked, then how are we yoked?

Note to Reader: Two Christians can be unequally yoked!

Oh my, how is that possible?!

Let's say a woman is a Christian, but she does not fully trust Jesus as Lord of her heart. She acknowledges Jesus as Savior and God the Father, but she does not know them intimately. In short, she does not trust Jesus' example to depend on God. And therefore, she does not understand His yoke is easier than any earthly yoke. In response to her life experiences, she chooses to carry her own yoke. For example, when faced with life trials, she self-medicates with alcohol, pills, and sex for relief, trusting this is the best option to handle her life problems. And the yoke gets heavier and increasingly ineffective.

And let's say a man is a Christian, but he has learned low self-worth and is terrified of poverty. He has more trust in his job than Jesus as Lord of his heart, so he is a workaholic to validate himself. He, too, is carrying his own earthly yoke rather than letting Jesus show him what is meant by 'My yoke is easy, My burden is light.

For both, they have given lordship (small 'l') to habits they trust more than Jesus habits. Their habits become cumbersome, and diminish their life spiritually, relationally, and mentally. But they continue to rationalize this is the way they are, and this is the life they accept.

They meet, date, and get married. And picture it.

Lord Jesus is not fully trusted in either of their lives. When trials come (that burden, that load), the wife turns to the yoke she is familiar with prior to marriage. So does her husband. It strains the marriage, and they pull apart. The yoke that is supposed to help them pull forward is weakened and is not effective. They may consider Jesus, but not as the top priority, not in a way beyond their limited ability, so they do not depend on Him much. They become stagnant because instead of moving the load forward together, they turn in the opposite direction, pulling away from each other, and weakening their partnership.

Maybe one of them gets tired of what is happening to their marriage. What if one of them decides to elevate Jesus, making Him Lord of their heart, turning to His example to deal with their problems?

Let's say the wife continues to self-medicate, but the husband decides to agree with Jesus's example and puts God first in his heart. He repents, and asks God's forgiveness, to cleanse, to let go of the past, and to start to move forward. He begins to seek counsel to understand why he became a workaholic. He commits to consistent bible study, daily prayer, and spending time with at least one godly and mature male friend.

His wife maintains her yoke with self-medication. So, the marriage is still unequally yoked currently. Picture it, again.

The gap is still there because the husband no longer sees Jesus on his level but has yoked with Jesus as Lord; but his wife has not decided to yoke with Jesus as Lord in her heart.

Some time passes, and the wife starts noticing a change in her husband. He is more available, he is more loving, he is much calmer, he is willing to assist her with getting the help she needs to heal. But she trusts her husband more than Jesus at this point, even though she is beginning to trust the self-medicating less. So, the yoking in the marriage is still unequal.

There is still a gap, though a different one. The yoke is still weakened because the woman has chosen to elevate her husband as lord in her heart over the self-medication. And because the husband has accepted Jesus as Lord of his heart, the yoke between he and his wife has a gap or fracture in it. They are still not in agreement or on one accord about who has lordship in the marriage. But the husband nor the wife is giving up.

He continues to yield to Jesus's Lordship, following the word of Jehovah God, praying, and following counsel he is receiving on how to love his wife. He continues seeking support for himself from a godly man (or godly men). Consistently.

This is a time of great transition, spiritual warfare, and it is HARD. Both are very vulnerable. The marriage may or may not last. As much as the husband wants to see his wife healed, she must agree and accept Jesus as Lord in her heart.

Let's say she says yes……

Now they both are agreeing to trust Jesus to carry their yoke. They actively trust His ways, and his example of leaning on God for all they need in every circumstance. They have decided to make knowing God intimately their highest priority as they live life together. And they begin to see the load of life they have become lighter, not because the trials stop coming, but because of WHO they now trust to lead them through these circumstances. It results in increasing understanding, forgiveness, respect, peace, joy, contentedness, growth, maturity, focus on godly purpose - the ingredients for a husband and wife who are friends, but more deeply, have unconditional and lasting love.

In hindsight, both will recognize the painful cost of not allowing Jesus to be Lord of their heart and yoke with him. They will know how close their marriage came to being destroyed. Both can see how the vices they allowed to be lord was a real threat and caused them to pull away from each other and Jehovah when facing life challenges. Both are now in position with Jesus at the center to help them in every way. Thus, He truly has the lightest yoke of all because He shows us how to trust and follow God in every way possible. Yep, this is being equally yoked.

Let's say the wife says no.....

The gaps continue to widen until the yoke is broken. The marriage is broken. Whether they divorce or not, two lives are separated.

One reason Jehovah says in His word 'Be equally yoked' is because He knows how deeply painful and difficult it is for two people, even Christians, who are unequally yoked, to live and stay as one. He prefers we not have that battle. He wants us to have the best journey possible as husband and wife, as He knows trials will come in this world.

Based on the two scenarios above, the marriage could have been successful or unsuccessful. The outcomes pivoted on the decisions each spouse made.

It is important to recognize signs of being unequally yoked as early as possible, to avoid the pitfalls. Some other relatable terms for unequally are......

Differing

Uneven

Disparate

Dissimilar

Distant

Divergent

Unbalanced

Mismatched

Not equal

If the yoke between the husband and wife is uneven, they are not in agreement about how to progress together, as a team, when faced with life challenges. These signs are also evident prior to marriage.

Scripturally, we can look at the verses that describe what equally yoked marriages are and understand the opposite of these qualities applies for unequally yoked marriages.

Simultaneously, the scripture, when directly addressing being unequally yoked, simply reinforces not to do it.

Amos 3:3 says, "Do two walk together, unless they have agreed to meet?" This scripture clearly confirms an agreement exists in relationships we have, including marriage, equally yoked or unequally yoked.

II Corinthians 6:14 says, "Don't team up with those who are unbelievers. How can righteousness be a partner with wickedness? How can light live with darkness?" This verse is quite interesting because it is an emphasis on different ways people are unequally yoked. Do you see it? Look at the first statement.

"Don't team up with those who are unbelievers." It's easy to assume this only means a Christian should not yoke with a non-Christian. However, earlier there was a Note to Reader: A Christian and Christian can be unequally yoked. Why? Because a Christian who has accepted Jesus as Savior but not as Lord in their heart has something else as lord of their heart. Hence, there is an unbeliever part of their walk that is still active and remains a primary influence of how they live their life. If they yoke with a Christian who has accepted Jesus as Savior and as Lord in their heart, the two are unequally yoked. This scenario is not uncommon.

Look at the next part of the verse. "How can righteousness be a partner with wickedness?" This question is less directed to the person, but to the fruits of the choices the person has made. Righteousness is consistent behavior because of a dependency on and intimate relationship with God. Wickedness is the opposite. It is the consistent behavior because of a lack of dependency and intimate relationship with God. In summary, the behaviors clash, and are not conducive to a fruitful partnership.

The next part of the verse is "How can light live with darkness?" There is no balance in the relationship under these circumstances because they are in opposition to each other. The light is analogous with life giving practices, the darkness is analogous to life taking practices. This creates an ongoing battle, one which weakens a marriage, and undermines any positive attributes in it.

Chapter 7

An argument is presented about the percentages of marriage which are not successful in the Christian church. Keep in mind, many believers are unequally yoked in marriage because of lack of understanding of the meaning of an equally yoked marriage. So, the equally yoked marriage at some point is not a primary goal, or a goal at all.

Simply, if it is a goal, there is not enough understanding on how to obtain it. Instead, the approach is fi guring out how to have a great marriage based on a variety of models - media depictions, peer expectations, chemistry, and a lot of guess work.

The lack of definitive understanding leads to unequally yoked marriages, and a high occurrence of divorce.

So, what exactly are qualities of an equally yoked marriage according to scripture, day to day?

There are many scriptures which describe it below.

God thought that it was not good for man to be alone. In response, He created woman to be with man. He said that a man should leave his mother and father, and join with his wife, and they shall become as one body, no longer just living for one. And what Jehovah has joined together, let nothing or anyone separate.

Related scriptures - Genesis 2:18; 2:23-25, Matthew 19:4-6

Wives are to submit (it means agree to position for success in the relationship, agree to encourage the leadership of the husband as he agrees to follow God's instructions; it does not mean to be a doormat) to their husbands. Husbands are to love their wives as Jesus loves the church (the body of believers is compared to the bride of Christ). Husbands are not to be harsh with their wives, seeking understanding with them, honoring her as a woman, treating her has a co-heir of Jehovah's grace, and so the husband's prayers will not be hindered.

Related scriptures - Colossians 3:18-19; 4:6, 1 Peter 3:7

The marriage bed is not to be defiled.

Related scripture - Hebrews 13:4

The husband and wife are together, a team. When one falls, the other will lift them up. The husband sees his wife as bone of my bones, and flesh of my flesh, as natural part of himself he does not want to live without her. Because of this need, he will hold fast to her, fight for her, protect her, sacrifice for her, work to provide for her, cherish her. He, as a bridegroom, will rejoice over her. God will rejoice over the union.

Related scriptures - Ecclesiastes 4:9-10, 12, Isaiah 62:5

The husband and wife are to have a consistent sexual relationship. They may agree not to have sexual relations for a period to focus on a special time of prayer, but this time should be limited to a range that is short enough to prevent them from being vulnerable to sexual temptation outside marriage.

Related scriptures - 1 Corinthians 7:2; 5ong of Solomon 2:16; 5:1; 5:9-10; 6: 4-6, 7; 8:6-7

The husband and wife are to communicate effectively with each other, showing their affection and appreciation for each other. The wife is inviting to her husband to enjoy her physically, mentally, emotionally. The husband expresses his desire to enjoy her and only her. Their affection and admiration for each other is open, real, and inspiring to those around them. They flirt with each other in private and public. They are attentive to and care for their physical and mental states. They hold each other in the same high esteem as close family.

Related scriptures - Ephesians 4:2-3, 4:32, 5:21-33; Colossians 3:19, 1 Peter 4:8, Proverbs 3:13-18; 4:23; 5:18; 10:12; 11:25; 12:4a; 16:3; 31:10-12

The husband pursues his wife before and during the marriage. He is consistent in his actions toward her. She is open to, expects, and encourages his pursuit. They agree with God that each is 'the one.'

They recognize their divine personal purpose, and they support each other in completing it. They enhance each other in fulfilling their individual highest calling, and this collaboration becomes a part of their purpose of a married couple.

Related scriptures - Mark 10:9, Psalms 85:10-11; Romans 8:28

They are close friends first, then lovers. They learn about each other intimately.

Related scriptures - 1 John 4:18, Matthew 19:6, 1 Thessalonians 3:12; 5:15-22, Philippians 1:9-10, II Timothy 1:7

Forgiveness of each other and repentance is a requirement in response to offenses.

Related scriptures - Psalms 51:10; 122:7; 1 Thessalonians 5:15-22

They respect each other.

Related scriptures - Philippians 2: 3-4; 4:4-9, James 1:19-20, John 13:34; 15:12, Titus 2:1-8, Romans 12:9-10, Joshua 1:9

In communication with each other, they apply lessons from Jesus's examples of consistently listening, hearing, and responding in sensitivity according to the word of God, His Father.

Related scriptures – John 4:5-26; Proverbs 20:5; James 1:19

Note to Reader. If you read any of the related scriptures above, you may notice some of them directly reference marriage. Several do not directly reference marriage because they are instructions for the individual, too.

And this is just a basic description, ground rules, of Jehovah's equally yoked marriage. The application of these instructions enables the marriage bond to deepen. And there is so much more in the scriptures about it.

Chapter 8

Th e equally yoked marriage is not a fairy tale. Not only is it obtainable, but it is also necessary for marriages to be authentic and lasting.

Some reader may be thinking, 'I don't even know how to date well, let alone get married, and be equally yoked!'

We can learn about the dating to marriage process through scriptures, too.

One scripture says "A man who finds a wife finds a good thing."

What does 'find' mean? Imagine a male reader asking this question: 'Does finding a wife mean I just hunt blindly for women? Does it mean I sleep with every woman I am attracted to until the chemistry is just right? Do I let my parent(s) choose a wife for me? Do I find a wife primarily based on the approval of my peers? Do I find a wife based on the woman who pursues me the hardest?'

The insight into 'a man finds a wife' is in Genesis and Song of Solomon.

Genesis 2:21-25

"So, Jehovah God caused the man to fall into a deep sleep, and while he was sleeping, he took on of his ribs and then closed the flesh over its place."

Man in a deep sleep is....

Relaxed

Vulnerable

Open to receive

Comfortable

Can be led

Wearing no mask

Jehovah God took one of his ribs. Why?

Well, look at the purpose of the rib cage. What is this rib cage thing all about? Why did Jehovah select this part of the man's body?

The rib cage protects the organs in the chest cavity.

Lungs

Diaphragm

Heart

The rib cage movement assists with breathing.

The rib cage provides support for the upper extremities. It is attached to the vertebral column.

During inspiration, the ribs elevate. During expiration, the ribs are lowered.

Whoa!!

The rib cage is bony.

From the uppermost part of the rib cage, it becomes more open. It is semi-rigid, but expands, able to increase in size. The small joints between the ribs and vertebrae permit a sliding motion of the ribs on the vertebrae during breath and other activities, for ease.

The first seven ribs in the rib cage are attached to the sternum by - costal cartilages. These ribs are called True Ribs.

The next three ribs - are called False Ribs.

The last two ribs in the rib cage have their cartilage ending in the muscle in the stomach wall and are called Floating Ribs.

The design of the lower five ribs gives freedom for the expansion of the rib cage and for ease in movement of the diaphragm.

From the description above, the words associated with the reason for the rib cage's existence.…

Protection

Assistance, with breathing, which necessary for life

Support

Elevation

Expansion

Make smoother

Freedom

Movement

True

Strong

WOW!

So which rib did Jehovah God pull from man while he was asleep? The scripture does not say, which is genius. Because the rib, whichever one it is, is reflective of the best woman for the man. Right? She is uniquely made, selected, and presented to the man by Jehovah. The man doesn't just blindly hunt or find a good thing in a wife. Jehovah creates a need and a longing for his wife internally, so when she is presented, he recognizes and can agree she is what is best for him, and he is what is best for her. And that's a really good thing!!

Are you asking how this longing, this need, is created? Good question. One way of explaining it is looking at what happened in the Garden of Eden before woman was created. Man was there, creation was there, Jehovah asked him to name all the creatures, and he did. He knew they were there as a part of Jehovah's plan to provide for him. So, this man was in relationship with Jehovah, obedient, responsive, working, and in unity with the creation around him. What was missing? His female complement. And this is where the longing for woman started.

Then Jehovah, in his infinite wisdom, responded to this need, this longing, this desire for woman. He said, "It is not good for man to be alone."

More questions about the rib? Good! Are you thinking there is one less rib in the man? Does the man function well before he is presented with woman, his rib? Meaning, can he still live, move, breathe, function.

Did the rib taken from the man grow back? Why didn't Jehovah just create woman without taking a rib from man?

Thanks to our knowledge of the body, we know that humans, male and female, have twelve sets of ribs, given there are no genetic defects that alter the body.

So, let's just assume Jehovah replaced the rib He took from man. That replacement is unique, needed, but still different from the one used to make woman. Because while they are both ribs, the purpose for each of them is not the same anymore. One is not meant to replace the other. And man knows something that was good, that was there in him from the beginning, changed. And he longs for it, even though he does well with the replacement.

Another consideration. Let's assume Jehovah took the rib from man, took from it what was necessary to make woman, which altered it, molded it so it would still work as a rib does in the body, and put it back. Only now the memory of what the rib was before will remain with man. And since it was good, and necessary, although he functions well, he knows something is different, and is missing. He longs for it.

Truth is, the scripture doesn't describe how Jehovah placed the rib in man again. However, the scripture is very clear about the connection Jehovah created between man and woman.

The removal of the rib, and the use of it to create a living being, woman, is a godly act, a miracle, only achieved by the Creator. And from this, their spirit, flesh, minds, and emotions can connect in every way, allowing a unique relationship, capable of being eternal. Jehovah planned for this union to last during life on earth, and with Him in eternity. He made it possible.

Chapter 9

So why isn't there a description of which rib Jehovah took from man to make woman? Possibly because the rib selected by Jehovah is specific for each man. Yes, the woman is custom made for the man, to be a match that pleases Jehovah. So, depending on the man, Jehovah selects the best rib (woman) of the twelve sets. The man's DNA, family history, his vulnerabilities, his destiny walk, his purpose, his physical strengths and weaknesses, his mindset, his tendencies, all are a factor in this process, but most importantly of all, his intimate relationship with Jehovah is necessary for this miracle of marriage to manifest. Where his heart lies......

And how does this benefit the woman? Since she is custom designed to match the man, she is valued in the highest way. She is the prize. What does this mean? Well, how does a man act when he not only values a woman in the highest way, but also knows he needs her to enhance his life?

He honors her.

He respects her.

He protects her.

He provides for her.

He longs for her in her absence.

He envisions his future with her.

He fights for her.

He sacrifices for her.

He listens to her.

He sexually desires her in a way that is unmatched for other women.

He wants and needs her in his life.

He wants her to be the mother of his children.

He wants her to be a part of his family.

Next to Jehovah, she is the priority.

How does the woman respond?

She agrees with being presented to him.

She does not pursue him.

She is authentic, and comfortable with herself.

She continues to live her divine purpose and expects him to complement it with his divine purpose.

She encourages him to move forward in friendship, relationship, and marriage with her.

She is like a rib – by supporting, assisting, affirming, protecting, make movements easier for the parts of man that are required for life.

How special and amazing this is!

So much, that man acknowledged. According to Genesis 2:23, "Then the man said, this one at last is bone of my bones, and flesh of my flesh. This one shall be called woman, for from man was she taken."

Note to reader: After man woke up (he realized, he accepted, he agreed), he KNEW she was a part of him.

And Genesis 2:24 emphasizes the connection between man and woman, husband, and wife:

"That is why a man leaves his father and mother and cleaves to his wife, and they become one flesh."

And there are scriptures which use the same word 'cleave' to describe the bond God desires with us. For instance,

Joshua 22: 5 says, "But take diligent heed to do the commandment and the law, which Moses the servant of the Lord charged you, to love the Lord your God, and to walk in all His ways, and keep His commandments, and to cleave to Him, and to serve Him with all of your heart and with all of your soul."

Deuteronomy 30:19-20 says, "This day I call the heavens and earth as witnesses that I have set before you life and death, blessings, and curses. Now choose life, so that you and your children may live and that you may love the Lord your God, listen to His voice, and cleave to Him."

Deuteronomy 4:4 says "But you that cleave to the Lord your God are alive, every one of you this day."

In context, the word cleave is to be loyal to, to cling, to stay bonded closely, to trust. The scriptures are full of promises of the benefits of this intimacy with God. And while the marriage relationship is different and secondary compared to the intimate relationship with God, the same word cleave is used to describe the intensity of the bond. It is meant to last, to deepen, and only God knows how to instruct us for this to happen.

Sometimes people do not believe this bond, this cleave, is possible between husband and wife. Not only is it possible, but it is also optimal for a man and woman to truly be united as a married couple, equally yoked, and stay together peacefully, fruitfully, healthily.

Funny, cleave also means to divide, as in separate from, or pull away. There are scriptures which use cleave to describe division from something that is life taking. Such as thoughts, practices, beliefs, values, vision, anything that would harm us or hinder our relationship with God. The willingness to do this is also a part of following Jesus's example to trust God instructions for our life. It is necessary to stay equally yoked in marriage.

This bond is a gift. There is no limit to how close a man and woman, husband, and wife, can become.

In fact, these are basic characteristics in the foundation of a marriage, as prescribed by Jehovah God.......

Adoration, Belief, Blessing, Commitment, Courage, Discernment, Encouragement, Endurance, Faithfulness, Favor, Forgiveness, Friendship, Fruitfulness, Generosity, Gentleness, Grace, Health, Hope, Humility, Integrity, Intimacy, Joy, Kindness, Love, Oneness, Peace, Protection, Provision, Purity, Purpose, Respect, Self-control, Servant Hearted, Strength, Submission, Thankfulness, Trust, Understanding, Value, Wisdom. (Taken from <u>40 Powerful Wedding Blessings to Pray Over Your Marriage</u>)[3]

And notice these are just BASICS. So, the marriage is not just limited to only the beautiful characteristics above. The potential is unlimited according to the word of God.

Does it seem the stories of the couples in the beginning of the book have been forgotten? Reader, they are not forgotten.

How far are you from being in an equally yoked marriage? Do you believe you can have a marriage that is equally yoked?

Before we go back to the couple stories shared earlier, here is a myth buster about the BEST MARRIAGE, an equally yoke marriage.

Man and Woman is perfect - a myth

As a single or married person, a man and woman have human weaknesses. To be equally yoked before and during marriage, the man and woman must be committed in their own relationship with Jehovah, and yoked to Jesus, agreeing He is Lord of your heart. This means trusting Jehovah above all with your heart, mind, body, emotions, and life. This means agreeing that you trust His son Jesus as your Lord in this earth and following the living example He gave. This commitment is evident and consistent, demonstrative. It means surrendering to the healing process needed for the best life – from our past trauma and drama. This process is not easy, very often uncomfortable, at times painful, sometimes frightening, but amazingly fruitful. It is required to be and stay healthy in an equally yoked marriage. We cannot do this solely by our own strength. But we can choose to trust the One who created the equally yoked marriage and follow His instructions to have and keep it (with His assistance, of course).

Chapter 10

Getting back to the couple stories

That **Couple 1** story, the one about the man in the second marriage. Over a period of a year, he decided to surrender everything – ego, pride, stubborn, temptations, self-righteous, money, career – everything he had not surrendered in his heart to Jehovah, and agree Jesus was Lord of his heart. He surrendered the yokes he was carrying. He agreed with Jesus to carry to the yoke.

His wife. She was almost totally disconnected from him, continuing to hold onto her limiting yoke. Until she consistently began seeing the changes described above.

In the early period of these changes, they remain separated, living apart, and he couldn't do much to persuade her he had transformed. It was extremely painful, in his words. But with the consistency and his steady yoking to Jesus, his husbandry increasingly reflected that of a man committed to being equally yoked with his wife, and she, after many months, responded by doing the same. Their marriage was reconciled, and they are now equally yoked.

Chapter 11

<u>Couple 2</u>

They are a powerfully, equally yoked couple-walking in and fulfilling their divine calling every day and content their marriage.

But let us take some time to look at another aspect of their relationship. When they married, they both had children from other marriages. The husband had children from each prior marriage. This is a blended family, and it is common. It is also particularly challenging, as there are multiple relationships impacting the marriage, primarily because of the bonds of the children and their biological and currently married parents.

A lot of scenarios are possible in blended families. In this case, the married couple is equally yoked. However, there are three other parents involved. Let's say they are all Christians, but the other three parents have not agreed to Jesus being Lord of their heart.

One of the parents (Parent 1) has remarried and is in an unequally yoked relationship. They also have another child.

One of the parents (Parent 2) is not remarried and has had two more children.

One of the parents (Parent 3) is not remarried, is hostile, resentful of this couple's marriage, and intentionally makes visitation with the children difficult.

This is a description of the magnitude of challenges surrounding this marriage. Why? Because relationships have dynamics, seasons, fluctuations, strengths, and weaknesses. If this couple attempted to be married and navigate all the trials of this family network without being yoked to Jesus in their hearts, they would soon find their marriage fractured deeply, and failing. However, in this marriage, they both agreed Jesus is the Lord of their hearts, and this agreement together gives them the day to day (sometimes moment to moment) successes in their relationship, their children, and their children's parents. As a result, the trials produce growth and blessing in their marriage. And they are an example of God's blueprint of marriage, how it profoundly and positively affects a husband and wife, their relationships, the past, present, and future. This is a powerful agent for blessing, healing, peace, longevity of life, unconditional love, and fulfillment of purpose for all involved. And this is just one married couple. Think of the multiple effects if most married couples agreed to be equally yoked.

Chapter 12

Couple 3

The husband was married before, but no children were born to the union. The wife had not married but had a child in her previous relationship. They were both very broken from the failure of these prior relationships. Both were Christians. Both wanted to marry again. They both gave Jesus Lordship of their heart.

To reiterate…

Both said they prayed fervently and consistently for their future spouse after their breakups. She said she prayed every day with a prayer partner and close female friend. They both said in response to their prayers, God gave them clarity about the characteristics of their future spouse, what they needed, and they were clear that their spouse had to align with their highest calling for God. Both knew soon after they met that they would marry.

They are equally yoked and flourishing as a couple and family.

This is also a great victory, a fitting example of equally yoked marriage. But it is good to look at them more closely – the period between a failed marriage and committed relationship, and when they met and married.

What was going on for the result to be so different and so much better than the previous relationships?

There was a time between their failed relationship and when they met and married another season of singleness for them. What was the difference between their single season this time, and their previous single season?

Both said after their last breakup, they were both heartbroken, but they both accepted that they were not in equally yoked relationships. They both realized they had not completed the single season prior to these relationships in a way that gave them the understanding of who they should be yoked with in marriage. Better said, they still did not grasp what it is to be equally yoked until after these failed relationships.

And a key response, they did not stop seeking God for the answers they needed. Actually, they dug deeper into consistent prayer, scriptural study for answers, being in relationship with others who supported their quest for understanding. They **allowed** God to prepare them for the spouse He wanted for them. They decided to agree with His plan, finally. God responded to both in many ways, well ahead of the time they met.

The wife, she speaks of daily prayer, bombarding God with her questions, concerns, and her requests of qualities for her future spouse. As she prayed daily, she began to visualize the God given husband, and her life with him. Yes, God was downloading her with His plan as she sought Him for answers. He began replacing her limited desire or even unhealthy desires for a spouse with His desires for the husband He wanted for her. It makes so much sense, because He created her, gave her the purpose for her life, so He knows what husband would align with her and her purpose in marriage. He knows the perfect match. And she finally agreed with Him. And when she met her husband, she recognized him, she saw him, she knew he was the ONE. Because spiritually she had already learned what to look for and accept, and she understood she would not compromise, rationalize, or talk herself out of the best for her. Or talk herself into less for herself with the wrong man.

And the husband. He sought God hard in prayer, too. Asking God to heal his heart from a failed marriage. Asking for guidance, correction. Asking for God to reveal his blind spots, to give him the courage and boldness needed to lead in a godly manner in the marriage he desired. Asking God to keep him focused so he would not choose a wife based on lust of the eyes, pride, or some external reason that would derail his goal of being equally yoked. And like Adam, and his future wife, he kept on living his purpose while he waited on God to present her. He saw her before he met her. He told his friends she was his wife. He knew. And after they started dating, when tempted to act in some of his old ways, God nudged him hard, and reminded him of what was changed in him. God made it clear he expected him to lead the relationship in the way he had matured in the prior single season – nothing less would do.

The husband agreed with God. He shared this revelation with his wife to be, and she agreed. A huge fork in the road moment for them. They married. They are equally yoked and thriving in their divine purpose. They are life giving and joyful couple to encounter, and a testimony to their loved ones, friends, and the world of that marriages like this – they are real, and within our reach.

God genuinely wants the spouse we pray to Him for to be the one we pray with throughout our courtship and marriage. It is required to have an equally yoked marriage to death do us part.

Chapter 13

In reflection, agreeing with God to have an equally yoked marriage, making the commitment to it, and living it is one of the most critical decisions one will make in life. While it is life giving, loving, fulfilling, adventurous, intimately satisfying, constantly growth provoking, and a foundation for unlimited generational blessings, it requires…

Routine and fervent prayer

Counsel from other equally yoked couple(s) and others (single persons included) who are equipped with the appropriate spiritual, wisdom, and life experiences to help uphold the union.

A supportive network of family and friends who hold the couple accountable to stay equally yoked

Consistent attention

An ever-growing friendship

Effective communication

Sacrifice

Humility (remaining teachable)

Consideration of your spouse just as much as, and sometimes more than yourself

Forgiveness

Each spouse making the other top priority, as family

Unconditional love

Respect

Education about different seasons in marriage and how they are navigated successfully

This is a labor of love. It is easy at times, and hard at other times. It is lasting. It is rewarding. It yields blessings which are lasting. It impacts a person's life at every level. It connects a person's life with the past and future. It is worthy of all it requires.

Chapter 14

In closing, a challenge to the Reader: Reflect on wedding vows. Yes, re-read them, say them, hear them, and live them with an understanding of an equally yoked marriage.

And remember these daily letter excerpts about Jehovah God's vows to us, taken from "Jesus Calling: Enjoying Peace in His Presence"[4]

Listen to the love song that I am continually singing to you. I take delight in you…I rejoice over you with singing. The voices of the world are a cacophony of chaos, pulling you this way and that. Don't listen to those voices; challenge them with My word. Learn to take minibreaks from the world, finding a place to be still in My presence and listen to My voice. There is immense hidden treasure to be found listening to Me. Though I pour out blessings upon you always, some of

My richest blessings have to be actively sought. I love to reveal Myself to you, and your seeking heart opens you up to receive more of My disclosure. Ask and it will be given to you, seek and you will find, knock and the door will be opened to you.

Continue on this path with Me, enjoying My presence even in adversity. I am always before you, as well as alongside you. See Me beckoning to you: Come! Follow Me. The One who goes ahead of you, opening up the way, is the same One who stays close and never lets go of your hand. I am not subject to limitations of time or space. I am everywhere at every time, ceaselessly working on your behalf. That is why your best efforts are trusting Me and living close to Me.

Trust Me one day at a time. This keeps you close to Me, responsive to My will. Trust is not a natural response, especially for those who have been deeply wounded. My Spirit within you is your resident tutor, helping you in this supernatural endeavor. Yield to His gentle touch; be sensitive to His prompting. Exert your will to trust Me in all circumstances. Don't let your need to understand distract you from My presence. I will equip you to get through this day victoriously, as you live in deep dependence on Me. Tomorrow is busy worrying about itself; don't get tangled up in its worry webs. Trust Me one day at a time.

∞Selah∞

ENDNOTES

[1]Oxford English Dictionary, 2023

<https://www.oed.com/public/home/home-page/>.

[2]Online Etymology Dictionary, 2001-2023

<https://www.etymonline.com/>.

[3]Debbie McDaniel, "40 Powerful Blessings to Pray Over Your Marriage", 04Oct.2016

<https://www.crosswalk.com/blogs/debbie-mcdaniel/40-powerful-blessings-to-pray-over-your-marriage.html>.

[4] Sarah Young, "Jesus Calling: Enjoying Peace in His Presence", 2004

www.ingramcontent.com/pod-product-compliance
Lightning Source LLC
Chambersburg PA
CBHW022052150726
47990CB00003B/1061